Accounting Basics

Dictionary

ALSO BY AUTHOR

Accounting Basics: Study Guide

The theory book in the *Accounting Basics* series, containing over 60 lessons on basic accounting concepts and practices.

Accounting Basics: Workbook

The companion workbook containing over 88 questions and exercises, which correspond to all of the lessons and chapters in the *Study Guide*.

Accounting Basics: Complete Guide

A compilation of the *Study Guide, Workbook* and *Dictionary* in a single *Accounting Basics* publication.

Accounting Basics

Dictionary

The companion dictionary of accounting and business terms
in the Accounting Basics series

MICHAEL CELENDER

Accounting Basics: Dictionary

ISBN 9781491269077

DEDICATION

This book is dedicated to my mom and dad.

Mom, if it were not for you I would have never had the education I had, or been able to tutor accounting at all. Thank you for your continuous support.

Dad, thank you for being a great teacher and showing me a different path.

ACKNOWLEDGEMENTS

I'd like to thank the following individuals for their assistance in producing this book, both those individuals and groups who directly helped with getting this book made and those that provided indirect assistance and support:

- Dr. Kobus Malan, who included me many years ago in a key accounting project and trusted me to draft high-quality educational materials for his college. His assistance resulted in my gaining valuable experience in developing accounting course materials.

- Zsuzsanna Kilián of Budapest, Hungary, for permission to use her image "Money Tower 1" for the front cover. The numerous other artists from *stock.xchng* (www.sxc.hu), who provided their images for use in the *Accounting Basics* series and on www.accounting-basics-for-students.com without any compensation. Also the creators of *stock.xchng* for providing such an invaluable free resource (a database of free images for use in various media).

- The Razzline community (www.therazzline.net) for their input and guidance in publishing this book and developing www.accounting-basics-for-students.com, including in particular Fred Hare and Dave Silberstein.

- Ken Evoy and his SiteSell team (www.sitesell.com) for providing a one-of-a-kind system for building and maintaining websites.

- L. Ron Hubbard for developing *Study Technology*© – in my opinion the best study system in the world and one that has helped me become a much better teacher and student.

Thank you all and may you reap the success you have graciously and unselfishly sown.

FOREWORD

L. Ron Hubbard states as part of his incredible study skills system, *Study Technology*[©], that you should *"be very certain you never go past a word you do not fully understand. The only reason a person gives up a study or becomes confused or unable to learn is because he or she has gone past a word that was not understood... This datum about not going past an undefined word is the most important fact in the whole subject of study. Every subject you have taken up and abandoned had its words which you failed to get defined."*

It is in that spirit that I wrote this accounting dictionary. I hope you use it to look up every accounting and business term you come across so that you progress in your studies and excel in accounting and business.

Please note that *Accounting Basics: Dictionary* is the companion dictionary in the *Accounting Basics* series of publications. Other books in the series include *Accounting Basics: Study Guide* (the theory book in the series) and *Accounting Basics: Workbook* (the companion book of questions and exercises). I would highly recommend obtaining the other two books in the series as these will ensure you have a thorough grounding in basic accounting. As an alternative you can also obtain *Accounting Basics: Complete Guide*, a compilation of the *Study Guide*, *Workbook* and *Dictionary* all together in one book.

Accounting basics are virtually identical the world over but occasionally there may be minor terms that differ depending on where in the world you are studying. The accounting and business terms presented in this book are fairly universal but some may be used more often in a particular part of the world. I would recommend to give priority to terms used in your accounting textbook or class notes and to ignore terms that are not relevant to you. In the end of the day you'll be tested on your accounting textbook or class notes, not on this book, right?

Sometimes a word may have multiple meanings. The definitions I have included here are specific to the accounting and business world. Other definitions for the same words can be found in regular dictionaries.

I have done my best to ensure this dictionary is as complete as possible. But I'm sure there are more terms that could be found and included. The business and accounting world is, of course, continuously evolving, and with that comes new words and phrases. Occasionally it may occur that you find a term that is not defined here. If so, make sure you look it up in a regular or business dictionary.

Here's to your future success in studying accounting!

Accounting Basics

Dictionary

ACB transfer – ACB stands for Automated Clearing Bureau, also known as an Automated Clearing House (ACH), which is a nationwide electronic network linking financial institutions (banks) for the purpose of facilitating electronic transfers of funds (source: www.scottstringfellow.com). An ACB transfer is a transfer of funds using this electronic network.

Account – 1) n. In accountancy, the summary record of all transactions relating to a particular item in a business, also indicating the item's current *balance*. This is also sometimes called a *T-account* due to its appearance.
2) n. A bank account is the *balance* of the cash deposited by a person at the bank, which can then be withdrawn by this person.
3) v. To *account* for something means to keep a record of something in your business by using the *accountancy* system.

Accountancy – The system of recording information about a business. This information is then presented to various people to help them make decisions. The information that is recorded and presented is primarily numerical. Also, the study of this recording system.

Accountant – The person in charge of collecting, recording, categorizing and presenting the accounting information of a business.

Accrual – 1) adj. *Accrual* describes amounts that have been accumulated and are still owed.
2) n. *Accruals* are *expenses* that have been *incurred* but have not yet been paid and are thus still owing.

Accrual basis of accounting – The accrual basis of accounting means that if a sale is made in October, but cash is received in January, the income is recorded in October (not when the cash is received in January). Between October and January we record that cash is owed (a *debtor* or *creditor* is recognized). The accrual basis means that income and expenses are recorded in the periods to which they relate, and not necessarily when cash is received or paid. See the *cash basis of accounting.*

Accrued – This means "is/are owed" or "*payable*" or "owing."

Accumulated depreciation – Accumulated depreciation is the accumulation of all *depreciation* charges per year up to a specific point in time. It is the negative part of the non-current asset. It is the asset's negative side – the total of the decreases in its value. It can be seen as the shadow account of the (positive) asset.

Accumulated profit – A *reserve* that is specifically used for the accumulation or retention of *profits.* Each year profits are first transferred into this reserve. Thereafter, funds can be transferred from this reserve to other reserves or to owners (as distributions). Reserves are the second component of *owner's equity*, after *capital.* A reserve, in common English, means something kept back or stored up, as for later use or for a special purpose. In accountancy, *profits* are retained (kept back) in *accounts* called reserves. Also known as *retained earnings* or *retained income.*

Allowance – An amount that the tax authorities allow you to deduct from your recorded income when determining how much tax you should pay over. This is basically another word for a *deduction.*

Amortization – *Depreciation* for *intangible assets* (e.g. computer software, trademarks, recipes, brand names, designs, etc.). See *depreciation.*

Appropriation account – A temporary *T-account* opened to facilitate distributions to owners (used in businesses that have more than one owner, such as a *partnership, close corporation* or *company*).

Asset – An *asset* is officially defined as "a resource controlled by the *enterprise* as a result of past events and from which future economic benefits are expected to flow to the enterprise." More simply, an asset is a possession of a business that will bring the business benefits in the future.

Asset disposal account – A temporary *T-account* opened specifically when an *asset* is disposed of (sold or scrapped). It is used to cancel the records of the asset in your business, to record money received for the asset from another (if it is sold) and to calculate a *profit* or *loss* on the sale or scrapping of the asset.

Asset register – A report showing a complete list of *assets* in your business as well as their values.

Audit – A process in which an *auditor* collects evidence in order to provide an opinion on whether the information presented in the *financial statements* of a business is accurate or not.

Auditor – The person in charge of certifying whether the information presented in the *financial statements* of a business (by the accountant), is reliable or not.

Auditor's report – A report by an *auditor* on the *financial statements* of a business, in which the auditor states how reliable the figures in the financial statements are.

Authorized share capital – The maximum number of *shares* that a *company* has been authorized to issue. Compare *issued share capital.*

Bad debts – These are debts to your business that have "gone bad." In other words, someone bought something from you on credit, and they agreed to pay you in future, and now you no longer expect them to pay you, so the debt has "gone bad" and you "write it off" as irrecoverable.

Balance – 1) n. The amount of an item at a point in time, *The balance in the bank account on the 1ˢᵗ of January was $5,000.*
2) v. To agree in value, *The debit and credit sides balance.*

3) v. To *balance a T-account* means to find its *closing balance.*

Balance sheet – A *statement* that shows the *balances* of *assets, liabilities* and *owner's equity.* The total of the *assets* must *balance* with the total of *equity* and *liabilities.*

Balance sheet accounts – *Balance sheet accounts* are *assets, liabilities* and *equity.* Compare *nominal accounts.*

Bank reconciliation – The process of *reconciling* the business records of its bank account with the records the bank has (as presented in the bank statement). Any differences are corrected either by adjusting our own records, or getting the bank to adjust their records. To get the bank to adjust their records, we send them a *bank reconciliation statement.*

Bill of lading – A written receipt issued by a carrier, a transport company, that it has taken possession and received an item of property, and usually also confirming the details of delivery such as method, time, place or to whom it will be delivered (source: http://duhaime.org).

Bond – 1) A loan from the bank where a piece of property serves as security in case the borrower cannot pay the bond payments.
2) A type of financial instrument issued by the government or by large corporations. It is effectively a loan to the government or corporation from the purchaser of the *bond.*

Bookkeeping – The practice of keeping up to date the *books,* or accounting records, of a business. Accounting records used to be kept manually (in books), but today they are mostly computerized.

Books – The accounting records of a business. Accounting records used to be kept manually (in books), but today they are mostly computerized.

Book value – The value of an *asset* according to the *books* (accounting records) of the business that owns it. This is not necessarily the amount that a buyer would pay for this asset, but rather the asset's value on paper according to the owner/s.

Bottom line – The *net profit* or loss a business is making. This term derives from the net profit or loss being the last line of the *income statement*.

Break-even point – To *break even* means to match the expenses one has already paid out (as part of starting and running a business) with income generated by the business. In other words, to make neither a profit nor a loss. The *break-even point* is the point at which the level of sales or other income exactly covers the business expenses. The break-even point helps managers determine the minimum amount they have to sell to (just barely) survive as a business.

Capital – 1) n. The investment of *assets* in a business by the owner or owners. This is the first category of *owner's equity*. The owner's stake in the business (*owner's equity*) increases when he invests *assets* in the business, because it is <u>his</u> assets (it is not owed to anyone else).

2) n. Money supplied to a business, whether this if from the owner or from long-term loans.

3) adj. The capital portion of a loan, as opposed to the interest portion, is the total of the loan excluding any interest that must be paid on this.

Capitalization issue – When a company wishes to pay *shareholders* a special bonus, it will issue more *shares* to existing shareholders… This means that shareholders will end up owning more shares (without having to buy them) and will receive *dividends* on these new shares together with the old ones (source: McGregor's Dictionary of Stockmarket Terms, Ryan, C., 1995).

Carriage – Transport costs.

Carrying amount – The amount at which we carry a *non-current asset* in our records. The carrying amount is equal to the cost of the asset less its *accumulated depreciation*.

Carrying value – The same as *carrying amount*.

Cash basis of accounting – According to the cash basis, if a sale is made in *October*, but cash is received in *January*, the income is recorded when the cash is finally received in *January* (not when the sale is made in October). We do not record any amount owing between October and January. See the *accrual basis of accounting.*

Cash book – A special *T-account* which shows all cash *receipts* and cash payments for you business. The cash book is really a combination of two *journals*: the *cash receipts journal* and the *cash payments journal*, yet is presented in the form of a T-account with receipts on the left and payments on the right.

Cash discount – This is a discount given to a client for paying their account promptly. This discount allowed is recorded as its own expense in a "discount allowed" account. Also known as a *settlement discount.*

Cash equivalents – These are short-term investments that are easily convertible to actual cash such as bank accounts and treasury bills (also called *bonds* – definition 2 above), and even checks that have not yet been deposited or cashed.

Cash float – Money kept on hand and used for minor expenses; *petty cash.*

Cash flow – A flow of cash (to or from a person or business).

Cash payments journal – One of the seven books of account. This journal is intended for all transactions involving the payment of cash, whether for expenses, assets, etc.

Cash receipts journal – One of the seven books of account. This journal is intended for all transactions involving the receipt of cash, whether for sales of goods, services rendered, sales of assets or anything else.

Check (also *cheque*) – A written order given to the bank to transfer cash out of one bank *account* and into another. The recipient of the cash will either be a person specifically named or the person who "bears" (presents) the check (called the "bearer").

Check counterfoil (also *cheque counterfoil*) – This is the part of the *check* kept by the *drawer* (writer) of the check as a record of the transaction.

Clearing account – A temporary *account* containing costs or amounts that will soon be transferred to another account. The *trading account* and *profit and loss account* are examples of *clearing accounts* (source: www.allbusiness.com).

Closing balance – An item's *balance* at the end of a period.

Closing transfers – *Journal entries* (a *debit* and *credit* entry) done at the end of the year to cancel out *incomes* and *expense* accounts and to transfer their value to another account like the *trading account* or *profit and loss account* (in order to work out *gross* or *net profit* respectively). The income and expense accounts are temporary accounts (called *nominal* accounts) that are cancelled out or brought back to zero at the end of each year.

Club – A *club* is a specific type of *non-profit organization* that normally involves an association of members. These members pay periodic fees (usually annual) so as to establish and maintain their membership in the club. A common example of a club is a country club, where members pay annual fees and in exchange can use the sporting and recreational facilities at the club premises.

Company – A *company* is a large business with a lot of *equity*, owned by tens, hundreds or thousands of owners (called *shareholders*). The owners own small parts of the company, called *shares*. There are two main types of companies, namely *public companies* and *private companies*.

Concern – In the field of commerce it means a business.

Consideration – In the field of commerce it means a payment for a product or service.

Consumables – Goods purchased in order to be consumed (used up) by the business itself (e.g. cleaning materials or stationery). Consumables are a type of *inventory*.

Contra account – The opposite account. The word *contra* means "against." If we debit "bank" and credit "capital," "capital" would be the contra account of "bank." "Bank" is likewise the contra account of "capital."

Control account – This is an account in the general ledger that summarizes all transactions associated with a specific accounting category. The most common examples of control accounts are the *debtors control account* and the *creditors control account*. The *debtors control account*, for example, would summarize all transactions with *debtors*.

Cost – The amount at which we first record an *asset* we have acquired (usually at the value of the cash given over).

Cost accounting – A specialized study and practice within *management accounting* that deals with the detailed analysis and control of costs and *revenues* so as to achieve greater *profits*. Cost accounting is particularly relevant to *trading* and *manufacturing* businesses. Compare *management accounting* and *financial accounting*.

Cost of goods sold – The original *cost price* of the goods that you have sold in *this* period. This is recorded as an *expense* in the period in which we sell the goods, and is compared to the value of your sales to determine a *gross profit*. Also known as the *cost of sales*.

CPI – The Consumer Price Index (CPI) is a measurement of the average general rise in prices of consumer goods and services taken as a whole (which includes food, housing, electricity and transportation), expressed as a percentage. The CPI represents *inflation* for consumers.

Cr – This is an abbreviation for the Latin word *credere* meaning "to trust" or "to believe." It has come to represent the *credit* side of an account or a credit *journal* entry. Credit means "right" or "right side" or "making an entry on the right side."

Credit – 1) Means "right" or "right side" or "making an entry on the right side." *I think you should credit the bank account.*

2) n. Referring to a *transaction* where money is lent. *I hope the bank will extend my credit.*
3) adj. Referring to a *transaction* whereby money is not paid straight away, but instead is owed. *I prefer credit agreements because I can pay later.*

Creditors – Also known as *payables*. The businesses and/or people that I owe. It also refers to the value of these debts as a whole. A creditor is a type of *liability*.

Creditors allowances journal – One of the seven books of account. This *journal* is intended for all transactions where there is a return of *inventory* originally purchased (on *credit*). Also known as the *purchases returns journal*.

Creditors analysis – A detailed report of all the *creditors* of the business including the value and age of each of these debts.

Creditors control account – This is an account in the *general ledger* that summarizes transactions with *creditors*.

Creditors journal – One of the seven books of account. This *journal* is intended for all transactions where there is a purchase of *inventory* on *credit*. Also known as the *purchases journal*.

Creditors ledger – This *ledger* only contains *accounts* for each person or business that our business owes (each *creditor*).

Current – Short-term. Describing an *asset* expected to be sold, or a *liability* expected to be settled (paid off) within a year's time from the current date.

Debit – means "left" or "left side" or "making an entry on the left side."

Debit order – An agreement between a business/individual, the bank and a third party to pay the third party a certain amount each month on a specified day of the month. The amount to be *debited* (decreasing your account from the bank's perspective) is determined by the third party each month.

Debtors – Also known as *receivables*. The businesses and/or people that owe me. It also refers to the value of these debts as a whole. A debtor is a type of *asset*.

Debtors allowances journal – One of the seven books of account. This *journal* is intended for all transactions where there is a return of *inventory* originally sold (on *credit*). Also known as the *sales returns journal*.

Debtors analysis – A detailed report of all the *debtors* of the business including the value and age of each of these debts to your business.

Debtors control account – This is an account in the *general ledger* that summarizes transactions with *debtors*.

Debtors journal – One of the seven books of account. This *journal* is intended for all transactions where there is a sale of *inventory* on *credit*. Also known as the *sales journal*.

Debtors ledger – This *ledger* only contains *accounts* for each person or business that owes our business (each *debtor*).

Declining balance method – A method of *depreciation* whereby the depreciation per year is based on the asset's carrying amount up to the beginning of that year. This is also known as the *diminishing balance method* or the *reducing balance method*.

Deduction – An amount that the tax authorities allow you to deduct from your recorded income when determining how much tax you should pay over.

Deficit – A *deficit* is a *loss* made by a *non-profit organization* or *club*. It is the opposite of a *surplus*.

Demand deposit – A bank *account balance* which can be drawn upon on demand, i.e. without prior notice (source: www.investorwords.com).

Deposit – 1) v. To place money in a place for safekeeping. *I will deposit some money in my account once I get paid.*

2) n. Something put in a certain place for safe-keeping. *I made a deposit of $500 in my account.*
3) n. Money paid as an initial amount that provides a guarantee that the full amount will be paid in the future or that something will be done in the future. *I paid a deposit of $50,000 on the new house.*

Deposit slips – Documents serving as proof that cash has been deposited in a bank account.

Depreciable amount – The amount subject to *depreciation*. This is usually the cost price, but if there is a *residual value*, the depreciable amount will be less. If you bought a machine for $1,000 and expect to be able to sell it 6 years later for $100 (the residual value), the depreciable amount is only $900 ($1,000 – $100). The depreciation per year in this example would be $150 [($1,000 – $100) / 6 years].If the residual value was $0, the depreciable amount would be the full $1,000 ($1,000 - $0). The depreciation per year would then equal $167 ($1,000 / 6). See *depreciation*.

Depreciable assets – These are *assets* that can or should be depreciated. In other words, *non-current* assets (apart from land and buildings). See *depreciation*.

Depreciable value – Same as *depreciable amount*.

Depreciation – *Depreciation* means a lessening in value. It is the decrease in the value of an *asset* over each of the years for which we use it to its final value. It is also the allocation of the full cost of the *asset* as a yearly *expense* over these same years. Depreciation is an *expense*.

Diminishing balance method – A method of *depreciation* whereby the depreciation per year is based on the asset's carrying amount up to the beginning of that year. This is also known as the *declining balance method* or the *reducing balance method*.

Direct labor – Labor directly involved in making the product, such as a mechanic. This includes people working with their hands or operating machines used to manufacture the product.

Direct materials – Key materials that are directly used in making the product. Also known as *raw materials*.

Directors – A company is run by the board of *directors*. The directors are appointed by the owners (the *shareholders*). The directors will in turn appoint managers to manage the company on behalf of the shareholders. Some directors may also act as managers of the company. In this case, they are called *executive directors*. Directors that are not involved in this day-to-day running and management of the business are known as *non-executive directors*.

Disclose – v. (in accounting exercises and questions) To prepare the notes to the financial statements in addition to the statements themselves.

Distributable reserves – See *reserves* for explanation.

Diversification – An *investment* or *portfolio* strategy designed to reduce exposure to risk by combining a variety of investments, such as *shares*, *bonds* and real estate, which are unlikely to all move in the same direction at the same time. Diversification reduces volatility in returns and allows for more consistent performance under a wide range of economic conditions. Diversifying (or not putting all your eggs in one basket) limits losses in the event of a decline in the value of your investment.

Dividends – The paying of *dividends* is the distribution of *profits* to the owners of a *company* (called *shareholders*) as a reward for their investing in the company.

Double-entry system – *Double-entry* literally means "two entries." The double-entry system means that, for each *transaction*, two entries are made by the *accountant*. This is the system in *accountancy* of recording a *debit* and a *credit* for each transaction.

Dr – This is an abbreviation for the Latin word *debere* meaning "to owe." It has come to represent a *debit* side of an account or a debit journal entry. Debit means "left" or "left side" or "making an entry on the left side."

Drawings – When the owner removes assets from his business, we call this *drawings*. This is because the owner *withdraws* assets. Drawings is the opposite of *capital*.

Duty – A charge on something, such as on imports.

Earnings – Earnings is the same as *net profit*.

Economic life – The estimated useful life of a *depreciable asset*. In other words, how long you expect to be able to use an asset before it becomes unusable.

EFT transfer – EFT stands for Electronic Fund Transfer, and is any transfer of funds that is initiated by electronic means, such as an electronic terminal, telephone, computer, ATM or *magnetic tape* (source: www.investorwords.com).

Electronic transfers – Transfers of money made by using the internet or other electronic means.

Enterprise – A business, usually one that has been started up despite various risks.

Equity – See *owner's equity*.

Estate – An individual's total possessions, especially all the property one owns at one's death.

Estimated useful life – The years you estimate you will be able to use an *asset* for. In other words, the number of years over which you will *depreciate* the asset. See *depreciation.*

Excess – A specified contribution towards the cost of an insurance claim, stipulated on certain insurance policies as being payable by the policyholder (source: Collins English Dictionary – Complete and Unabridged 6th Edition 2003).

Exchange – A place where financial instruments, such as shares in a company, are exchanged or traded (bought and sold).

Excise and customs duty – *Excise* is an internal tax imposed on the production, sale, or consumption of a commodity or the use of a service within a country. *Customs duty* is a duty (charge) or tax imposed on imported and, less commonly, exported goods (source: www.thefreedictionary.com).

Expenses – Events that result in money flowing out of the business. An example of an expense is vehicle repairs.

Fair value – The amount a willing, knowledgeable and unconnected person would pay for an asset in the ordinary course of business (a related party, such as a family member, would often have to pay less than an unconnected party).

Financial accounting – *Financial accounting* is the study and practice of keeping and maintaining historical accounting records for a business and the presentation of this information in the form of *financial statements* to external business *stakeholders* such as *shareholders* and *creditors*. Compare *managerial accounting.*

Financial statements – Financial statements are the most important reports of a business. These statements are prepared from the information in the trial balance. The purpose of these statements is to show the reader the *financial position*, *financial performance* and cash flows of a business, as well as various other useful information concerning it. Financial statements consist of (amongst other things) an *income statement*, *statement of changes in the owner's equity*, *balance sheet*, *cash flow statement*, notes to these various statements and (where needed) an auditor's report. Financial statements are usually prepared once a year.

Financing – The act of getting money (to spend on *assets* or *expenses*). Financing also means where you get your money from. Financing is the source of money. It can be obtained from the owner (*capital*) or from a lender (such as a bank *loan* – in other words, from *liabilities*). Financing can also be obtained internally from the *profit* or *income* that you make.

Finished goods – *Inventories* that have been fully manufactured and are ready for sale. An example of this would be a table.

Fixed asset – The same as a *non-current asset.*

Fixed costs – Costs, such as rent, which do not vary but are instead a fixed amount. For example, each month the rent comes to $2,000. Compare *variable costs*.

Fixed deposit – An *account* (like a savings account) opened at a bank for a fixed term or that requires a set notice period from the customer to access the funds. For example, a 30-day deposit requires that you give notice to the bank 30 days before you can withdraw the funds.

Fixed installment method – Another name for the *straight line method* of depreciation. In this method the depreciation per year is based on the *asset's* original cost, resulting in a constant depreciation charge each year.

Folio number – The folio number is a cross-referencing code. It cross-references between one document and another, such as between the journal entries and the accounts (the next step). The folio numbers make it simple to trace information through the steps in the accounting cycle.

Forensic audit – The application of accounting methods to the tracking and collection of forensic evidence, usually for investigation and prosecution of criminal acts such as embezzlement or fraud. Also called forensic accounting (source: www.businessdictionary.com).

Fraud – The intentional deception of another person, resulting in the loss (to the other person) of property or some right.

Freight in – Transport costs for goods coming in to a business. This *expense* actually forms part of the total cost of acquiring the *asset*.

Freight out – Transport costs for goods sent from a business to the customer. This expense is not set off against sales but rather is recognized as a general business expense in the *income statement*.

Friendly society – An association of people who join together for a common financial or social purpose. The members often pay regular fees towards insurance, sickness benefits, savings, old age pensions, etc. (source: www.wikipedia.org).

GAAP – Generally Accepted Accounting Principles. A widely accepted set of rules, conventions, standards, and procedures for reporting financial information (source: www.investorwords.com).

Geared – When one says that a business is highly *geared*, it means that it funds a lot of its *assets* or investments through borrowed funds (debt) instead of through the owner's *capital* (*equity*). See *gearing* below.

Gearing – *Gearing* is the amount of purchases or investments paid for with borrowed funds (debt) or the act of using debt to pay for purchases or investments so as to achieve greater gains. The greater the gearing, the greater the possible gain or potential loss. It is measured by the ratio of a company's debt (*liabilities*) to its *equity* (source: American Heritage New Dictionary of Cultural Literacy, Third Edition). Also known as *leverage.*

General journal – The general journal is a *journal* (book of account) comprising all entries that are not recorded in the other journals. Examples of these entries are year-end adjustments.

General ledger – The general ledger is our main *ledger*. Virtually all *T-accounts* in a business fall under this ledger.

General reserve – A type of *reserve*, without any specific purpose, and from which distributions to owners can be made. Reserves are the second component of *owner's equity*, after *capital.* A reserve, in common English, means something kept back or stored up, as for later use or for a special purpose. In accountancy, *profits* are retained (kept back) in *accounts* called reserves.

Goods Received Voucher – A document serving as evidence of the receipt of goods.

Gross – means "before deducting…"

Gross margin – The gross margin is the ratio of the *gross profit* to the selling price on the *inventory* that a trading business sells. For example, if a business sells shoes for $30 each and they cost them $20 each, then they make a gross profit of $10 per pair of shoes. The gross margin here is $10/$30, which equals 33.3%. In other words, they make 33.3% profit on the selling price of each shoe. This is a standard percentage, based on the selling price, which a business uses to work out a *gross profit*. Also known as the *gross profit percentage*.

Gross profit – The profit calculated before taking into account (before deducting) our general business expenses. Gross profit is calculated by deducting the *cost of sales* from our *sales*. It can be thought of as an initial *profit* on the product we are selling.

Gross profit percentage – The gross margin is the ratio of the *gross profit* to the selling price on the *inventory* that a trading business sells. For example, if a business sells shoes for $30 each and they cost them $20 each, then they make a gross profit of $10 per pair of shoes. The gross margin here is $10/$30, which equals 33.3%. In other words, they make 33.3% profit on the selling price of each shoe. This is a standard percentage, based on the selling price, which a business uses to work out a *gross profit*. Also known as the *gross margin*.

Hedge funds – An investment fund usually used by wealthy individuals and institutions. To *hedge* means to protect against loss or to manage risk. Hedge funds are exempt from many of the rules and regulations governing other similar funds, allowing them to trade using a variety of instruments and use complex investment strategies. They are restricted by law to no more than 100 investors per fund, and as a result most hedge funds set extremely high minimum investment amounts, ranging anywhere from $250,000 to over $1 million (source: www.investorwords.com).

Hire-purchase – An agreement between a seller and buyer whereby the buyer takes possession of the asset on paying a deposit and thereafter continues to make regular payments (installments), while the seller retains ownership of the asset until the final installment is paid. The buyer can make use of the asset while paying it off.

IAS – Stands for *International Accounting Standards*. IAS were issued between 1973 and 2001 by the board of the International Accounting Standards Committee (IASC). In April 2001 its successor, the International Accounting Standards Board (IASB), adopted all IAS and continued their development, calling the new standards IFRS (source: www.thefreedictionary.com).

IFRS – Stands for *International Financial Reporting Standards.* These are international accounting standards (policies). Many of the standards forming part of IFRS are known by the older name of *International Accounting Standards* (IAS). IAS were issued between 1973 and 2001 by the board of the International Accounting Standards Committee (IASC). In April 2001 its successor, the International Accounting Standards Board (IASB), adopted all IAS and continued their development, calling the new standards IFRS (source: www.thefreedictionary.com).

Imprest amount – The imprest amount is the amount of cash needed on a monthly basis for the *cash float* or *petty cash.* It is the start-up amount for the petty cash box.

Income – The event that results in money flowing into the business. A sale is a common form of income.

Income statement – A *statement* showing the *profit* or *loss* that a business has made during a certain period. A more appropriate name for this could be "profit statement."

Income tax – The tax charged on your income and paid over to the tax authorities. In most countries income tax is progressive, i.e. people who earn more pay more tax. Also known as *normal tax.*

Incremental – Means additional. The term is often used when a business is considering new projects or changes in operations. When making a decision to go ahead with these ventures or not, the business looks at the *incremental* cash inflows and outflows (or *incomes* and expenses) associated with the new project or change in operations in contrast to cash inflows and outflows (or incomes and expenses) that are already occurring.

Incur – To incur a debt or *expense* means to cause the debt or expense to exist for one's business.

Indirect labor – This is the cost of personnel not directly involved in manufacturing the product, but whose cost forms part of the general business expenses of the factory (the factory *overheads*). Included in this is wages and salaries to factory supervisors, cleaners and security guards. Indirect labor is recorded separately from *direct labor*, and falls under the category of *overheads*.

Indirect materials – Inventories that are used in the manufacturing process but whose cost is insignificant. For example, in manufacturing a car, the nuts, screws and bolts would be indirect materials. Cleaning materials that are consumed in producing a completed, clean car would also fall under indirect materials. Indirect materials are recorded separately from *direct materials*, and falls under the category of *overheads*.

Inflation – The continuous, general rise in the prices of goods and services. *Inflation* can occur because of an increase in general demand (more people want more products, so producers can raise the prices), an oversupply of money (so that money is now not really as valuable as before so producers now have to raise the prices to get the same value for selling their goods) or simply by producers simply raising their prices.

Insolvent – Describing a business that cannot pay all its debts. If a business is *insolvent*, it means that the total debts of the business are greater than its *assets*.

Installments – A series of regular payments made to pay off a debt.

Intangible assets – *Assets* that cannot be physically touched or felt but that have monetary value. Examples of intangible assets are brand names, patents, computer software, recipes and designs. Brand names or logos such as Nike or Coca-Cola are intangible assets. These names (and their accompanying designs) cannot be touched like a building or machine, but they still have significant value.

Interest – 1) A share or portion of something. For example, "I have a 40% interest in this business."

2) A charge by the bank (or other lender) for the lending of money over a certain period of time. It represents the value (for the lender) of not having the money for a certain period. The interest charge is calculated using a percentage rate of interest based on the loaned amount. For example, a loan of $100,000 may have an 8% interest rate per year. This means that the lender will pay $8,000 of interest for a year.

Inventory – Goods that you own. *Inventory* can be sub-classified into *merchandise* or *consumables*, as well as raw materials, work-in-progress and finished goods (for a manufacturing business).

Investing – The spending of money. But to spend money one would need to have it first. Thus one would always need *financing* to occur first before engaging in any *investing* activities. One can spend money on (invest in) things that provide only immediate benefits (*expenses*), or in things that provide benefits that last for a long time (*assets*).

Investments – In accounting, investments are *assets* that are purchased and kept over a period of time with the purpose of providing a return (without any work performed on or with the asset). Examples of investments are savings accounts (that accumulate *interest*), *shares* in a *company*, buildings or paintings that increase in value over time, etc.

Invoices – Documents listing goods or services provided, as well as their prices. Suppliers normally sends an invoice together with goods (or once services have been delivered) so as to indicate the amount of payment required to be paid to them. In addition, invoices often indicate how soon the payment is to be made, the business banking details, etc. Invoices thus normally relate to credit transactions.

Issued share capital – The number of *shares* (and its total value) that a *company* has actually issued (sold) to the public. Compare *authorized share capital.*

Journal – A chronological (date-order) record of *transactions* entered into by a business. Journals are your first basic entry of *debit* and *credit* for a transaction. Their purpose is simply to keep a day-to-day record of a business and its transactions. Journals are also the different books of account. There are seven of these books: the *cash received journal, cash payments journal, sales journal, sales returns journal, purchases journal, purchases returns journal* and *general journal.*

Lease – There are two types of leases, a *finance lease* and an *operating lease.* An *operating lease* is an agreement where one person rents an *asset* from another person in exchange for a regular payment of cash. The ownership of the *asset* does not pass to the person renting it, but is still owned by the original owner when the agreement comes to an end. A *finance lease* also involves installments (regular payments), but in this case the ownership of the asset does pass to the other person (from the start of the agreement).

Ledger – A *ledger* is a number of T-accounts grouped together. It is the collective term for the *accounts* of a business. (A ledger of accounts is like a school of fish).

Legal tender – A country's currency (legally valid currency) that must be accepted as payment for a debt (source: www.investorwords.com).

Leverage – *Leverage* is the amount of purchases or investments paid for with borrowed funds (debt) or the act of using debt to pay for purchases or investments so as to achieve greater gains. The greater the leverage, the greater the possible gain or potential loss. It is measured by the ratio of a company's debt (*liabilities*) to its *equity* (source: American Heritage New Dictionary of Cultural Literacy, Third Edition). Also known as *gearing.*

Liability – A *liability* is officially defined as "a present obligation of the *enterprise* arising from past events, the settlement of which is expected to result in an outflow from the enterprise of resources embodying economic benefits." Another definition for a liability is that it is simply a debt of the business. The debt will result in *assets* (usually cash) leaving the business in future.

Liquidate – To *liquidate* an *asset* is to convert it into cash (see *liquidity* below). To *liquidate* a business means to terminate the business by selling its *assets* (often at a reduced price) for cash and using this cash to repay debts and the owners (for their original investment in the business).

Liquidity – The ability of a business to convert its assets into cash quickly. Money, like liquid, flows quickly. If a business is liquid, it can convert assets to cash quickly. *Current assets* like *inventory* and *debtors* are very liquid. *Non-current assets* like land and buildings, or vehicles, are not very liquid because they take a while to sell and convert to cash.

Loss – The negative amount you are left with when your *expenses* exceed your *income*.

Management accounting – The study and practice of analyzing and interpreting internal accounting records and statistics by managers so as to make day-to-day decisions about the business. *Management accounting* also involves the budgeting of future costs and revenues and the estimating of costs and revenues for future investments and projects so as to decide whether or not to undertake these investments and projects. Also known as *managerial accounting*. Compare *financial accounting*.

Manufacturing business – *Manufacturing* means to make a product, whether by hand or by machine or both. A manufacturing business is a business that makes a *profit* primarily from producing goods and selling them to others at a higher price. The word *manufacture* comes from Latin *manu facere* which means "make by hand" (*manus* = hand and *facere* = to make).

Margin – The profit on something or the value by which the selling price of an asset exceeds its cost.

Marginal – *Marginal* describes amounts that are new or additional. This is often due to a change in operations or a new project, etc. Marginal amounts are in contrast to amounts that would be spent (or received) regardless of whether the business changed its operations or invested in the new project or not – *expenses* or *incomes* that were being spent or received already. Thus a *marginal cost* is a new or additional cost brought about by a new project or a change in operations, etc. *Marginal* *income* is the new or additional income brought about specifically by a new project or a change in operations, etc.

Market – A place where *assets* are traded. Also, a collective term for all the buyers and sellers where the *asset* is traded.

Market capitalization – The total value of all the listed *shares* of a public *company*. For example, if a company has 1,000,000 shares currently trading at $105 per share, their *market capitalization* is $105,000,000. The market capitalization figure gives a good indication of the value of a company.

Market value – The value of an *asset* according to the *market*. *Market value* is the average, agreed-upon value for an *asset* as determined by general trading (buying and selling).

Mark-up – The *mark-up* is the amount one "marks" the cost up by to get to the selling price one is charging. For example, if it costs you $1 to purchase a cold drink and you sell it for $1.50, the *mark-up* is $0.50. The *mark-up* can also be represented as a percentage. In the above example the mark-up (in percentage terms) is 50% - $0.50 mark-up divided by $1 cost price.

Merchandise – Goods purchased for resale. Merchandise is a type of *inventory*.

Money market – A *market* for short-term financial instruments, which are generally very safe investments and which return a relatively low interest rate (source: www.investorwords.com).

Mortgage – An agreement whereby a person borrows money to buy property, especially a house, and the lender (usually a bank) may take possession of the property if the borrower fails to make regular payments (installments). The word originates from Old French and literally means "dead pledge" – from *mort* dead and *gage* security. The house or other property acts as security for the loan and the house can be *dead* for the owner if he or she does not make its loan payments.

Negotiable instrument – A written, signed promise or order to transfer a specified sum of money to another person. Examples of *negotiable instruments* are *checks* and promissory notes (source: www.teachmefinance.com).

Net – means "after deducting…"

Net asset value – The value of *assets* after deducting assets that will be used to pay *liabilities* (debts) – in other words, the assets the owners of the business really own and do not owe to external parties. This is, in essence, another name for the *owner's equity*. The net assets represent the net worth of a business according to the *balance sheet* values.

Net assets – The value of *assets* after deducting assets that will be used to pay *liabilities* (debts) – in other words, the assets the owners of the business really own and do not owe to external parties. This is, in essence, another name for the *owner's equity*. The net assets represent the net worth of a business according to the *balance sheet* values.

Net margin – The net margin is the ratio of the *net profit* to the total sales. For example, if a business sells shoes for $50 each and their expenses are $40 each, then they make a net profit of $10 per pair of shoes. The net margin here is $10/$50, which equals 20%. In other words, they make 20% net profit on the selling price of each shoe. Also known as the *net profit percentage.*

Net profit – The *profit* calculated after taking into account (after deducting) our general business expenses and tax expense. Net profit is calculated by deducting the general business expenses and tax expense from our *gross profit.*

Net profit percentage – The net profit percentage is the ratio of the *net profit* to the total sales. For example, if a business sells shoes for $50 each and their expenses are $40 each, then they make a net profit of $10 per pair of shoes. The net margin here is $10/$50, which equals 20%. In other words, they make 20% net profit on the selling price of each shoe. Also known as the *net margin.*

Net realizable value – This represents the amount of cash that you expect can be *realized* (obtained) from the sale of the *asset* (if you decided to sell it) less any estimated selling costs (such as sales commission) and costs necessary to complete the sale (such as petrol/fuel costs for delivering the asset).

Net sales – The final sales figure calculated after deducting from sales the total of sales returns.

Nominal accounts – *Nominal accounts* are *income* and *expense accounts*. *Nominal accounts* can be contrasted with *balance sheet accounts*. Whereas *balance sheet accounts* are permanent accounts that show the *financial position* of a business (*assets*, *liabilities* and *equity* – the accounting equation) and whose *balances* accumulate over years, *nominal accounts* are temporary accounts whose *balances* accumulate only until the end of the year, at which point they get restarted at zero for the next year. Remember that *income* and *expenses* (*nominal accounts*) are used to calculate *profit*, and that this *profit* is calculated at the end of each year for that year. The *profit* shows the *financial performance* of the business for that year. At the beginning of the next year the *nominal accounts* start off with a balance of zero. This is done in order to restart the process of calculating *profit* for the next year. Because *nominal accounts* are temporary accounts, one could say that they are not "real accounts" (like the permanent *balance sheet accounts*), but rather exist only "in name."

Non-current – Long-term. Describing an asset expected to be sold, or a liability expected to be settled (paid off) beyond a year's time from the current date.

Non-profit organizations – These are organizations, such as welfare and educational organizations that do not exist so the owner makes a profit, but for other reasons, such as benefiting the community or a group of people.

Non-distributable reserves – See *reserves* for explanation.

Normal tax – The same as *income tax*.

Notice deposit – A savings *account* where the account holder is required to give a notice of withdrawal a specified number of days before making the withdrawal to avoid penalties. Also called *notice account*. (source: www.businessdictionary.com).

Opening balance – An item's *balance* at the beginning of a period.

Ordinary shares – These are *shares* in a *company* that do not have preferential rights (*preference shares* have preferential rights in comparison to ordinary shares). Ordinary shares, however, entitle the ordinary shareholder to voting rights in relation to the company, while preference shares do not. Additionally, dividends (distributions) paid on normal shares vary each year, while dividends on preference shares are a fixed amount. Compare *preference shares.*

Other financial assets – This is another term for the investments belonging to your business.

Outsource – To use an outside business to perform a certain function of your business (they become the source of this function).

Overheads – The running costs of a business. Examples of overheads include water and electricity, rates and taxes, and insurance for a building or vehicles.

Owner's equity – The *owner's equity* is officially defined as "the residual interest in the *assets* of the enterprise after deducting all its *liabilities*." It is the owner's share of the assets of a business. Owner's equity, often just called *equity*, represents the value of the *assets* that the owner can lay claim to (i.e. the value of all the assets after deducting the value of assets needed to pay liabilities). It is the value of the assets that the owner <u>really</u> owns.

Overdraft – A facility (service option) to draw over (beyond) the cash one has in a bank account, thus creating a *liability* towards the bank.

Overheads – General business expenses (apart from the expense of purchasing *raw materials* and of employing *direct labor* such as factory workmen). Examples of overheads are rent on the factory, insurance on machines, and water and electricity.

Par value – The *par value* of a *share* is the value assigned to a share by the issuing company when first issued. The par value of a share bears very little relationship to its actual value (*market value*).

Partnership – A *partnership* is a business relationship between at least two people. The partners (the owners of a partnership) agree to run a business amongst themselves for the purpose of making a profit for each of them. The partners share in the profits (and losses) made by the business according to an agreement. Each partner contributes towards the success of the business and is also personally liable for its debts. The partnership does not exist as a separate legal liability. The partners thus pay tax in their own names on their portion of partnership profits.

Payable(s) – 1) n. Also known as *creditors*. The businesses and/or people that I owe. It also refers to the value of these debts as a whole. A payable is a type of *liability*.
2) adj. "To be paid," "is/are owed" or "is owing." For example, "The debt is *payable*."

Periodic inventory system – This is a system that does not involve keeping continuous, moment-to-moment records of *inventories*. Most small businesses have a periodic system of records for inventory. Where one does periodic inventory counts (such as once a month, or at the beginning and end of each year), and does not have an accurate record of the inventories in between these points – well, this is a periodic system. Compare *perpetual inventory system*.

Perpetual inventory system – Perpetual means <u>continuous</u>. This is a system where a business keeps continuous, moment-to-moment records of the number, value and type of *inventories* that it has at the business. Electronic accounting systems that are linked to each item of inventory are usually perpetual. For example, products that have barcodes are automatically recorded as having been sold at tills in a supermarket when they are "swiped." Inventory levels are automatically decreased as soon as the invoice has been electronically entered. Compare *periodic inventory system*.

Petty cash – A sum of cash on hand kept to pay small expenses. Also known as a *cash float*.

Petty cash book – A separate *T-account* for recording *petty cash* movements. It is presented in the same format as the *cash book.*

Petty cash journal – An additional *journal* (book or record of account) apart from the seven books of account. This journal is intended for all transactions involving payments made using petty cash, and cash receipts that have been included in petty cash.

Portfolio – A collection of investments all owned by the same individual or organization (source: www.investorwords.com).

Post – To *post*, in accountancy, means to transfer the information calculated in the *journals* to the various *T-accounts* in the *ledgers.*

Preference shares – These are *shares* in a *company* that have preferential rights, namely that preference *shareholders* get paid *dividends* (distributions) before ordinary shareholders, and that, upon termination of a company, the preference shareholders would get repaid their investment before the ordinary shareholders. Ordinary shares, however, entitle the ordinary shareholder to voting rights in relation to the company, while preference shares do not. Additionally, dividends (distributions) paid on normal shares vary each year, while dividends on preference shares are a fixed amount. Compare *ordinary shares.*

Present – v. (in accounting exercises and questions) To display. When one is asked to present *financial statements*, the examiner is normally asking you to merely draw up the *financial statements* without accompanying notes.

Private company – A *private company* is a company that is exclusive and is not available to the general public for investing purposes. As a result, a private company normally has far less *shareholders* than a *public company*. Compare *public company.*

Pro-forma – *Pro-forma* literally means "for form's sake" in Latin and describes a document created as a formality or as part of the established procedures, forms or rules. A pro-forma *invoice* is an invoice issued before an order is placed or before the goods are delivered, giving all the details and the costs of the goods, and used to confirm the order. It is not the same as the actual final invoice sent to the customer.

Proceeds – Cash from a *transaction*. In particular, *proceeds* are the cash received from the sale of an *asset*.

Profit – The positive amount you are left with when your *income* exceeds your *expenses*.

Profit and loss account – A temporary *T-account* opened at the end of the year to calculate the business *net profit*.

Profit motive – A person starts a business, and invests his *assets* in the business, so that the business will produce a *profit* for him. This reason or motivation of starting and running a business with the objective of making a profit, is called the *profit motive*.

Profitability – The condition of being profitable or how profitable something is.

Proprietary – This describes something that is privately owned or owned by a sole owner. A *proprietor* is an owner.

Proprietorship – *Proprietorship* means the ownership of something and in business is often refers to a *sole proprietorship* (a business with a sole owner who also runs the business).

Provision – A provision is a *liability* that will definitely occur but whose timing or amount is uncertain. What happens is that one knows one is definitely going to have a certain *expense* or *loss* in the future, such as a *loss* in the values of your stock (due to damage or theft) in the coming year (one is certain of this as it has occurred every year in the past). But one is not exactly sure how much of a *loss* there will be, or whether it will occur throughout the year, only in certain months, etc. So one makes an estimate of the future loss and calls this a provision. The word provision is from the Latin word *provisionem*, which comes from another Latin word – *providere*. *Pro-* means "forward" and *videre* means "to see."

Public company – A *public company* is a *company* that any member of the public can invest in. Public companies have their *shares* available to the public by trading them on a *stock exchange* The major purpose of the public company structure is to attract *capital* (invested funds) in large amounts through this public offering of shares.

Purchase orders (or requisitions) – These are *source documents* showing a requested amount and value of supplies either from another department or section within your business or from a supplier (external to your business).

Purchases – The account used to record the purchase of *inventory* when using the *periodic system* of accounting for inventory. *Purchases* is an *expense* account. It forms part of the *cost of sales* calculation at the end of the financial period.

Purchases journal – One of the seven books of account. This *journal* is intended for all transactions where there is a purchase of *inventory* on *credit*. Also known as the *creditors journal*.

Purchases returns journal – One of the seven books of account. This *journal* is intended for all transactions where there is a return of *inventory* originally purchased (on *credit*). Also known as the *creditors allowances journal*.

Railage – An amount charged for transporting goods by rail (source: www.dictionary.com).

Raw materials – *Inventories* that have not yet been used in the manufacturing process at all. An example of this would be a plank of wood.

R/D check – R/D stands for "<u>R</u>eturn to <u>D</u>rawer." The *drawer* is the person who writes (draws) a check. A check that has been returned to drawer means that the drawer's bank account does not have enough cash to pay the amount indicated on his check.

Realize – 1) To realize an *asset* means to sell the *asset* and receive cash.
2) To realize a *profit* means to gain or obtain a *profit*.

Rebate – A deduction from an amount to be paid or a return payment of part of an amount already paid.

Receipt – 1) A document confirming that cash or goods have been received.
2) A receiving of something.

Receivables – Also known as *debtors*. The businesses and/or people that owe me. It also refers to the value of these debts as a whole. A receivable is a type of *asset*.

Reconcile – To bring two differing groups or ideas into agreement or harmony. In accountancy, it specifically means to make two amounts agree in value.

Reconciliation – A calculation whereby one works out how one amount can be *reconciled* (made to agree) to another amount. In doing this calculation, one indicates the differences between each of the original calculations of the two amounts.

Reducing balance method – A method of *depreciation* whereby the depreciation per year is based on the asset's carrying amount up to the beginning of that year. This is also known as the *declining balance method* or the *diminishing balance method*.

Register – An official list or schedule or a book containing an official list or records.

Remittance advice – This is a document listing *invoices* needing to be paid, usually created and presented to a financial manager at the end of the month before he or she authorizes a supplier payment. This document can also be sent to suppliers together with the payment to show which invoices are being paid as well as any errors corrected in these invoices.

Reserves – This is the second component of *owner's equity*, after *capital*. A *reserve*, in common English, means something kept back or stored up, as for later use or for a special purpose. An example of this would be a reserve of food kept in the pantry. Army officers keep reserves of ammunition for when there is a battle. In accountancy, *profits* are retained (kept back) in *accounts* called reserves. Distributions of profits to the owners are made from the reserves. There are two kinds of reserves: *distributable reserves* and *non-distributable reserves*. Distributable reserves are reserves from which profits can be distributed to owners. Examples of these are *retained earnings* and the *general reserve*. Non-distributable reserves are reserves from which profits are not allowed to be distributed to owners. The most common example of a non-distributable reserve is the *revaluation reserve*, which contains profits arising from the revaluation of property (such as land and buildings).

Residual value – The amount you estimate you can sell an asset for at the end of its *estimated useful life*. For example, you buy a machine for $1,000 and estimate its useful life at 5 years. At that point you think you can sell it for $100. This $100 is its *residual value*. See *depreciation*.

Retained earnings – *Earnings* means *profits*. *Retained earnings* is a *reserve* that is specifically used for the accumulation or retention of *profits*. Each year profits are first transferred into this reserve. Thereafter, funds can be transferred from this reserve to other reserves or to owners (as distributions). Reserves are the second component of *owner's equity*, after *capital*. A reserve, in common English, means something kept back or stored up, as for later use or for a special purpose. In accountancy, *profits* are retained (kept back) in *accounts* called reserves. Also known as *accumulated profit*.

Retained income – The same as *retained earnings*.

Revaluation reserve – A *reserve* made up of *profits* on the revaluation of property (land and buildings) or on the revaluation of investments. *Dividends* (distributions to owners in a *company*) cannot be paid out of this reserve.

Revenue – Your main source of *income*.

Salary slip – A document showing the amount of your salary as well as any deductions in calculating this amount, such as for medical aid or for retirement funds, etc.

Sales discount – This is a discount given by a wholesaler to a retailer. It is granted so the retailer can buy the product at a relatively low price and make a *profit* when selling the product.

This discount is not recorded as its own expense in the accounting records, but instead is simply subtracted from the sales price before the sales value is recorded. Also known as a *trade discount.*

Sale and leaseback – An arrangement in which one party sells a property to a buyer and the buyer immediately *leases* the property back to the seller. This arrangement allows the seller to make full use of the *asset* while not having *capital* tied up in the asset. Leasebacks sometimes provide tax benefits (source: www.investorwords.com).

Sales journal – One of the seven books of account. This *journal* is intended for all transactions where there is a sale of *inventory* on *credit*. Also known as the *debtors journal.*

Sales returns journal – One of the seven books of account. This *journal* is intended for all transactions where there is a return of *inventory* originally sold (on *credit*). Also known as the *debtors allowances journal.*

Security – 1) A financial instrument such as shares in a company, which is traded on a *stock exchange* or *securities exchange.*
2) When it is agreed that a certain *asset* will be paid over if a loan is not paid off, the *asset* forms the *security* for the loan and its repayment. This asset *secures* against non-payment of the loan.

Sequestrate – To take and hold (property) by judicial authority, for safekeeping or as *security* (for the payment of a debt), until a legal dispute is resolved (source: Webster's New World College Dictionary).

Settlement discount – This is a discount given to a client for paying their account promptly. This discount allowed is recorded as its own expense in a "discount allowed" account. Also known as a *cash discount.*

Share – A *company* is divided into tens, hundreds or thousands of portions of *equity*. These portions of the company are called *shares*. *Financing* for a company is obtained primarily by offering shares to investors. These shares are "sold" to investors, and the company then receives *capital*, which it uses to fund its operations.

Shareholder – The person that holds a *share* in a *company*. The shareholder, through his or her shares, owns a part of a company. A single shareholder can hold one share, or can hold a thousand shares. Note that the shareholders (the owners) are not the managers and do not have to be managers at all. There can, in fact, be a fair distance between the shareholders (owners) and the management of a company. The shareholders appoint the board of *directors* to run the company.

Shareholders for dividends – A *liability* (debt) *account* representing the total amount of *dividends* (distributions of *profits*) owing to *shareholders* (the owners of the *shares* of a *company*).

Shareholding – The number or percentage of shares that a shareholder holds in a company. For example, Mr. Jay has a shareholding of 50,000 shares (out of 100,000 shares), or he has a shareholding of 50% in the company.

Sole proprietorship – This is also known as a *sole trader*. *Proprietorship* means ownership. Thus a sole proprietorship or sole trader is a business owned (and usually run) by an individual. A sole trader or proprietorship is the common business structure chosen for a small business. The advantage of a sole trader is that it is the most simple and uncomplicated business structure. At the same time the owner is wholly responsible for any business debts.

Sole trader – Same as *sole proprietorship*.

Solvency – This is the ability of a business to pay all its debts. When a business has far more *assets* than debts, its solvency can be said to be good. When it has more debts than assets, the opposite is true.

Solvent – Describing a business that can pay all its debts. In a solvent business, its *assets* are greater than its total debts.

Source document – A source document is the document, such as the cash slip, *invoice*, etc., that is the "source" of a transaction. In other words, it is the first document that exists relating to the transaction.

Stakeholder – A person who holds a stake in your business. In other words, changes in your business may have an effect on them, and they are thus interested in how your business performs. Your stakeholders may include employees, customers, suppliers and lenders, amongst others.

Standard costing – This is an accounting system making use of *standard costs*, which are predetermined target costs that the business aims to achieve under efficient operating conditions. Actual costs are compared to standard costs and variances are established. Standard costing is used mainly by manufacturing businesses.

Statement – 1) A report.
2) A specific report showing the amount owed by one business to another, as well as details of transactions between the two businesses.

Stock – 1) The total amount of inventory or goods on hand in a store or factory, etc.
2) Shares in a company.

Stock exchange – A public market where *shares* and other investments are traded (bought and sold).

Stock-holding list – A list of all the *stock* that your business holds, including types of stock and their respective values.

Stock-take – A counting and recording of the stock (*inventory*).

Stop order – An agreement between a business/individual and the bank to pay a third party a certain amount each month on a specified day of the month.

Straight-line method – A method of *depreciation* whereby the depreciation per year is based on the asset's original cost, resulting in a constant depreciation charge each year. Also known as the *fixed installment method*.

Subsidiary ledgers – "Subsidiary" means of lesser importance, or supplementing or supporting something else. Subsidiary ledgers are *ledgers* that support the *general ledger*, which contains most of the business accounts. Two common subsidiary ledgers are the *debtors ledger* and the *creditors ledger*. These two ledgers contain an individual account for each *debtor* or *creditor* of the business respectively (such as Mr. Jones or DFD Electronics, etc.).

Sundry – This word means "various," "miscellaneous" or "general." A *sundry* column is often used in *journals* to group together and show all items and amounts that are small or insignificant.

Suretyship – *Suretyship* is *security* (def. 2); a pledge or formal promise made to secure against loss or non-payment of a debt. *Suretyship* also refers to a person who agrees to pay a sum of money or to perform some duty or promise for another in the event that the first person fails to do so (source: www.thefreedictionary.com).

Surplus – A *surplus* is a *profit* made by a *non-profit organization* or *club*. It is the opposite of a *deficit*.

T-account – In accountancy, the summary record of all transactions relating to a particular item in a business, also indicating the item's current *balance*. This is called a *T-account* due to its appearance.

Taxable income – Taxable income is the final calculated amount on which you are taxed after listing one's income and subtracting from this any applicable *deductions* that you qualify for.

Trade discount – This is a discount given by a wholesaler to a retailer. It is granted so the retailer can buy the product at a relatively low price and make a profit when selling the product. This discount is not recorded as its own expense in the accounting records, but instead is simply subtracted from the sales price before the sales value is recorded. Also known as a *sales discount*.

Trading account – A temporary *T-account* opened at the end of the year to calculate the business *gross profit*.

Trading business – A business that makes a *profit* primarily from buying goods at a low price and selling them at a higher price.

Transaction – An exchange of goods or services between two parties.

Trial balance – A sheet displaying all the *accounts* of a business, drawn up as a trial (test) of whether the total of all the *debit balances* equal the total of all the *credit balances*. This sheet is prepared as a final check just before the *financial statements* are drawn up.

Unit trusts – A collective investment consisting of underlying *securities* (such as *shares*) that have been apportioned to unitholders in a trust fund. The underlying securities are managed by collective investment managers and investors on behalf of all the investors who share ownership of the pool of *assets* (the fund).

Useful life – The period of time, usually in years, that you expect an *asset* can be used in your business.

Variable costs – Costs, such as *raw materials* or labor costs used to make a product, which *vary* according to the quantity used. For example, if you want to produce more tables, you will require more wood (raw material). If you pay $1 per plank of wood, and use 4 more planks of wood to make an extra table, your cost (for the extra wood) will increase by $4. Compare *fixed costs*.

VAT – *Value-Added Tax*. This is a tax that is added to the value of most goods or services that are sold or rendered. It is called Value-Added Tax because it is a tax on the "value" a business has "added" to the product being sold or the service being delivered. In other words, if a business bought sweets for $5 and sold them for $7, it added $2 value. Or if it sold sweets for $7 and it cost $5 to make them, then the business again added $2 of value. This "added value" of $2 is taxed at a certain percentage and paid over to the tax authorities. The burden for this tax in actuality does not fall on businesses but rather falls on the consumer when he or she purchases goods or services. In the example above $7.70 (for example) would be listed as the price and included in this would be the extra $0.70 VAT (on top of the $7). The customer cannot claim the $0.70 back from the tax authorities. The business would pay over this $0.70 to the tax authorities.

Withholding tax – This is not a separate tax on its own, but a method of collecting tax. The tax is withheld by the party that is paying money out and then paid over to the tax authorities on behalf of another. For example, each month a portion of an employee's salary is withheld by the employer or business and paid over as tax to the tax authorities on behalf of the employee. This is an example of withholding tax and is also known as *employees tax*.

Working capital – The investment in the *current assets* of a business. The most significant working capital items are *inventory*, cash and *debtors*. Current assets result in the continued operation of the business (we sell inventory for cash or on credit). Thus *working capital* is the amount of the investment to keep the business running or working. *Net working capital* is calculated by subtracting *current liabilities* from *current assets*, and shows the *working capital* funded through actual long-term *capital* (not through short-term *liabilities*). The term *working capital* has thus also come to include reference to current liabilities in addition to current assets.

Work-in-progress – *Inventories* that have started the manufacturing process but that are not yet *finished goods*. An example of this would be a table with two legs. Also known as *work-in-process*.

Year-end – A year-end, in accounting, is the accounting procedure one does at the end of the year. It generally involves calculating the *gross* and *net profit* for the year and determining the *financial position* of the business.

ABOUT THE AUTHOR

Michael Celender is an expert in accounting and business education. He graduated with a bachelor's degree from Rand Afrikaans University (now the University of Johannesburg).

Michael has lectured and taught hundreds of students and developed a range of accounting courses in his native land of South Africa, including basic accounting courses for publication by a national media corporation (the "It's My Business" series of online courses published by Johnnic Communications), government accounting courses for the Accounting Standards Board and the Institute for Public Finance and Auditing as well as various college-level accounting and business courses.

After his degree he trained in *Study Technology*©, a revolutionary study system that gives educators the tools to teach with more clarity. Using this system he found that most, if not all, accounting textbooks did not explain the basic terms, concepts and procedures of accounting adequately. Seeing this "missing link" (and a few others) in existing literature, Michael decided to create his own, and the result is a comprehensive—and comprehensible—book on basic accounting concepts and practices, to help the average accounting student truly understand and excel at the subject.

———————————

www.ingramcontent.com/pod-product-compliance
Lightning Source LLC
Chambersburg PA
CBHW071642170526
45166CB00003B/1394